Deer Hunting

Sloan MacRae

PowerKiDS press.

New York

Published in 2011 by The Rosen Publishing Group, Inc.
29 East 21st Street, New York, NY 10010

First Edition

Editor: Amelie von Zumbusch
Book Design: Greg Tucker
Photo Researcher: Jessica Gerweck

Photo Credits: Cover, pp. 6, 7, 8, 9, 11, 12–13, 14, 15, 16, 20, 23, 24–25 Shutterstock.com; p. 4 Charles Ommanney/Getty Images; p. 5 Fotos & Photos/Getty Images; p. 10 PhotoLink/Getty Images; p. 17 Scott Markewitz/Getty Images; p. 18–19 Mike Kemp Images/Getty Images; p. 21 © www.iStockphoto.com/Tony Campbell; p. 22 © www.iStockphoto.com/Kriss Russell; p. 26 www.iStockphoto.com/Lauri Patterson; p. 27 Livia Corona/Getty Images; pp. 28–29 © www.iStockphoto.com/Paul Tessier.

Library of Congress Cataloging-in-Publication Data

MacRae, Sloan.
  Deer hunting / Sloan MacRae. — 1st ed.
      p. cm. — (Open season)
  Includes index.
  ISBN 978-1-4488-0710-9 (library binding) — ISBN 978-1-4488-1381-0 (pbk.) — ISBN 978-1-4488-1382-7 (6-pack)
  1. Deer hunting—Juvenile literature. I. Title.
  SK301.M29 2011
  799.2'7652—dc22
                              2010010700

Manufactured in the United States of America

CPSIA Compliance Information: Batch #WS10PK: For Further Information contact Rosen Publishing, New York, New York at 1-800-237-9932

Contents

School's Closed for Hunting Season!

Many people think about deer when they hear the word "hunting." This big, beautiful animal is by far the most hunted game in North America. Deer hunting has a rich history there, too. Deer were valuable to Native Americans because even a single deer provides a lot of meat. One kill could feed a small group of people for a long time. Deer also provided leather

This young hunter is headed out on her first deer hunt. Deer hunting is popular with hunters of all ages.

These petroglyphs, or rock carvings, show deer hunting. They were made thousands of years ago by Native Americans in what is now Utah.

for clothing, and their antlers were used to make tools.

Today we continue to hunt deer because of the challenge that hunting these fast, watchful animals provides. The sport remains so popular in the United States that some areas celebrate the first day of rifle season as a holiday. Hunters are free to take the day off from work and school.

White-Tailed Deer and Mule Deer

Deer and their relatives are hunted all over the world. Some big-game animals, such as caribou, elk, and moose, are also in the deer family. The males of this family all have antlers. These are sometimes mistakenly called horns. Horns are **permanent**, but

Antlers, such as the pair on this white-tailed deer, grow quickly. They are made of bone and are covered with skin and hair, called velvet.

Hunting Facts

Make sure that you see antlers before you shoot. It is often illegal to kill female deer.

Male deer, such as the ones shown here, use their antlers to fight over which ones will get to mate with females.

antlers fall off in winter or early spring. The males grow new antlers every year.

You have probably seen antlers hanging on a wall. They make excellent **trophies**, especially big antler racks with lots of points. You can count antler points simply by observing the number of branches on the rack. Hunters can win prizes for shooting the deer with the most points.

The most hunted animal in the United States is the white-tailed deer. It can be found in almost every state, and it also lives in Canada and Mexico. The white-tail is very common in mid-Atlantic states such as Virginia, West Virginia, and Pennsylvania. It is sometimes called the Virginia deer. It is the official state animal of several states, including Pennsylvania. White-tails often weigh up to 250 pounds (113 kg).

This buck, or male deer, is a white-tailed deer. As all deer do, white-tailed deer eat plants.

Female deer are known as does, while babies are called fawns. This doe and fawn are mule deer.

White-tailed deer may be big, but mule deer are even bigger. These deer live in western states, such as Colorado. They often weigh in at 300 pounds (136 kg). That is a lot of meat! When you shoot a mule deer, you might need some help dragging it out of the woods.

This large male deer is a mule deer. Mule deer are named for their large ears, which look a bit like the ears of mules.

One of the reasons that deer hunting is so common is that deer can live almost anywhere. They can be found in forests, fields, swamps, and farm country. Deer are most active around the time of sunrise and sunset. It is a good idea to be in your

Sunrise is a great time to hunt deer. This deer hunter is making his way across a field in the early morning.

Hunting Facts

Most states' hunting permits let hunters kill only one deer each season. Depending on the deer population, though, you can sometimes get extra permits to hunt additional deer.

This white-tailed deer is standing in a field. You can see the early morning light on the deer and the grasses around it.

deer-hunting spot before the Sun is up. Shoot only if there is enough light to see clearly, though.

To go deer hunting, you must have a hunting **license** that proves you have passed your state's firearm safety program. Most deer hunters wear their licenses pinned to the backs of their jackets. Each state has different hunting laws, and they can be confusing. Make sure you know your state's laws. You can usually find them on the Web site of your state's game **agency**.

Blaze Orange

The color orange can be a hunter's best friend. Deer have good vision, but they do not see colors the same way humans do. Orange jumps out to the human eye, but it is not nearly as visible to deer. Most states require hunters to wear bright orange to protect them from other hunters. While they cannot recognize colors as we do, deer do see patterns. Hunters often wear orange **camouflage** patterns to blend in.

Deer are challenging **quarry** because they have strong natural **defenses**. They have excellent vision,

This deer hunter's orange vest and hat will make him easy for other hunters to see. This shade of orange is often called hunter orange or blaze orange.

hearing, and senses of smell. They are also very fast, which means they are hard to shoot once their senses warn them of danger. Hunters can purchase special scents to mask their own smells and draw game to them. Think of these as perfume for deer!

Bullets and Slugs

Deer are big animals. It takes a powerful weapon to hunt them. Most deer hunters use rifles. These are long firearms that are held tightly against the shoulder. Rifles fire long, slender bullets that can travel hundreds of yards (m) and cause serious harm

Some hunters have ammo, or ammunition, holders on their guns. This rifle's ammo holder has room for several rifle bullets.

Hunting Facts

Always keep your rifle's safety on until you are ready to fire. Be mindful of the direction your firearm is pointing at all times.

This deer hunter is using a rifle. The thing he is looking into is a scope. Scopes are commonly used with rifles. They help hunters aim their guns.

to their **targets**. You should always handle them with care.

Rifles are too powerful to use in some areas. Certain kinds of rifles are outlawed in several states. It is dangerous to hunt with rifles near **suburban** communities. This is where shotguns come in handy.

Unlike rifles, shotguns are not made to shoot single bullets. Instead, they scatter small pellets, called shot. It is also possible to load shotguns with single shells, called slugs.

Slugs do not travel as far as bullets, but they do more harm than shot.

If you hunt deer with a shotgun, make sure it is loaded with slugs. It is illegal to hunt deer with shot because it is unlikely to kill cleanly. You will most likely only wound the deer and cause it unnecessary pain.

The hunter shown here is using a shotgun. If you hunt deer with a shotgun, remember to use slugs, not shot.

Bow Hunters

Hunters who prefer a greater challenge hit the woods during archery season. This is a special season when hunters are permitted to hunt only with bows. Archery is one of the oldest forms of hunting in the world. Modern compound bows can shoot farther and with more **accuracy** than the ones the Native Americans used.

This hunter is using a compound bow. As you can see in the picture, compound bows have many more parts than old-fashioned bows do.

However, even with these new bows, archery is not easy. Bowstrings are no match for firepower, and arrows do not fly as far as bullets. Archery hunters must be able to get closer to deer than hunters using firearms do. They rely on camouflage and scents in order to do this.

Some states have archery seasons that permit hunters to go without blaze orange. This is permitted only in archery seasons that do not overlap with other seasons. However, the deer archery season sometimes occurs at the same

Bow hunters need to get extra close to deer, so they must put lots of thought into choosing the spot from which they hunt.

time as turkey season. When this is the case, it is important for bow hunters to wear orange so that turkey hunters can see them. Otherwise, another hunter could shoot a bow hunter by mistake!

Hunting Facts

Archery hunters use special arrowheads called broadheads that are made especially for hunting deer.

Silence and Patience

Silence is golden, especially when hunting deer. There are several different methods for successful hunting, but they all require hunters to be as quiet as possible.

One deer-hunting method is to find a good spot and sit there patiently. How can you tell if a spot is good? Look for deer tracks and game trails. Deer tracks are easy

These footprints were made by a deer. Before you set out on a hunt, try to learn the tracks of animals that live in the area.

This mule deer has come to a stream to take a drink. Figuring out the places where deer might find food or water will help you find deer.

to spot if you know what to look for. Game trails are small paths that animals use when traveling through a forest. Seeing these paths is a good sign that deer have moved through the area.

Some deer hunters use tree stands. These are platforms in trees. You can think of them as small tree houses for hunters. Tree stands offer good views of the area. Hunters often hunt with blinds. These are screens that hide the hunters from deer.

Sitting still requires patience. It is not for everyone. Another successful method is to stalk, or still-hunt, deer. Still-hunting is the art of moving slowly, carefully, and

There are many kinds of tree stands. This hunter's simple tree stand is basically a seat that can be attached to a tree trunk.

This hunter is looking for deer on a snowy day. If you go hunting in the snow, remember to dress warmly.

quietly through the woods. It requires hunters to pay absolute attention to their surroundings. They must not wear clothing that makes noise. They keep their eyes open for animal tracks. Snow can play an important **role** in hunting, whether for good or for bad. Snow can help hunters see animal tracks, but a fresh snowfall will hide tracks.

Some blinds, such as the one shown here, are built on raised platforms at the edge of the woods.

23

Sighting In

Practice your shooting before the hunting season begins. This is especially important when using a new rifle. Many sporting clubs have shooting ranges. There, you can practice shooting from different positions. You can even buy targets that have pictures of deer.

Most hunters put scopes on their rifles. These tools magnify faraway objects. Scopes have targets, or crosshairs, to help you aim. You place the crosshairs exactly where you want to shoot. Good hunters try to kill deer as cleanly as possible. They do not want animals to suffer.

This hunter is sighting in his rifle at a shooting range. Sighting in your gun and learning how to use a scope are important if you want to hunt with a rifle.

You will need to sight in your rifle before taking it hunting. This makes sure that your rifle and scope are actually aiming at the exact same spot. Scopes come with instructions that tell you how to do this.

Venison

Congratulations! You shot your trophy buck. All that hard work and practice paid off. Unfortunately, your work is not yet done. The first thing you must do is tag your deer. The tag is a form on your license. Fill out the form, and put it on your

This venison was grilled and is being served with wild mushrooms. There are many ways to prepare venison.

Hunting Facts

Deer provide lots of meat. Some hunters donate their kills to organizations such as Hunters Against Hunger. The meat is then given to hungry families.

deer. Next you must clean, or field dress, your kill. This is absolutely necessary if you do not want your **venison** to spoil. Always remember to bring a sharp knife, rope, plastic gloves, and garbage bags.

Some butchers specialize in preparing deer. They can make venison steaks, **jerky**, and even ground venison for hamburgers and sloppy joes. You will also want to saw off the deer's antlers so that you can hang them on your wall.

Hunters sometimes have the heads of the deer they killed stuffed so that they can be hung on a wall. Stuffing animals is known as taxidermy.

Too Much of a Good Thing

It might seem strange, but hunting is actually good for deer as a **species**. In lots of places, deer no longer have many natural predators. This leads to unhealthy populations. Too many deer compete for a limited food supply. Large deer populations also create unsafe driving conditions. You have probably seen dead deer that were hit by cars on the side of the road. Having too many deer also causes problems for farmers because large deer populations destroy crops.

Deer hunters, such as this man, have played a big part in making sure that the wild areas where deer live are protected.

Today deer hunters fill an important role in many **ecosystems** by controlling deer populations. The government even hires hunters when population levels get too high. This is much safer than using poisons to do the same job. Most deer hunters love nature and are proud to help maintain its balance.

Happy Hunting

- ⊕ Be quiet! Remember that deer have very sharp hearing.

- ⊕ Be sure of your target before you shoot. Does the deer have antlers?

- ⊕ Bring some rope. You will need it to haul a big buck out of the woods.

- ⊕ Bring binoculars.

- ⊕ Make sure you know your state's hunting laws and seasons. They can be confusing!

- ⊕ Be extra careful on the first day of rifle season. There are a lot of hunters in the woods, and that means a lot of shooting.

- ⊕ Make sure you dress warmly when you go hunting. Bring gloves that allow you to grip your gun or bow safely.

- ⊕ Make sure your tree stand is secure. You do not want to fall out!

- ⊕ Scout your area and become familiar with it before the season starts. You do not want to get lost!

- ⊕ Pay attention at all times. It would be embarrassing to miss a trophy buck because you were daydreaming.

Glossary

accuracy (A-kyuh-ruh-see) The quality of being exactly right.

agency (AY-jen-see) A special department of the government.

camouflage (KA-muh-flahj) A color or a pattern that matches the surroundings and helps hide something.

defenses (dih-FENTS-ez) Features of living things that help protect them.

ecosystems (EE-koh-sis-temz) Communities of living things and the surroundings in which they live.

jerky (JER-kee) Strips of dried meat.

license (LY-suns) Official permission to do something.

permanent (PER-muh-nint) Lasting forever.

quarry (KWOR-ee) Something that is being hunted.

role (ROHL) A part played by a person or thing.

species (SPEE-sheez) A single kind of living thing. All people are one species.

suburban (suh-BER-bun) Having to do with an area of homes and businesses that is near a large city.

targets (TAHR-gits) Things that are aimed at.

trophies (TROH-feez) Animal parts that hunters save to show others after kills.

venison (VEH-nuh-sun) The meat from a deer.

Index

Web Sites

Due to the changing nature of Internet links, PowerKids Press has developed an online list of Web sites related to the subject of this book. This site is updated regularly. Please use this link to access the list: www.powerkidslinks.com/os/dh/